That Book on
Big Data
A One-Hour Intro

Jonathan Morley
Bobby Timberlake

TABLE OF CONTENTS

INTRODUCTION

Big data is an incredibly large field! Given the level of attention the topic has received in both industry and academia, amongst the press, and from friends, family, and colleagues, we decided to put together a guide for anyone who wants to get up to speed quickly.

The purpose of this book is to act as a one-hour survey course rather than a deep dive, and we'll touch on each of the moving parts that collectively come together to make "big data." We hope to provide a base level of knowledge and serve as a springboard if you're interested in learning more. By the end of this book, you should be ready to join the conversation, understanding where your company and data fits into the various ecosystems; what others are doing in the space, new and old; and a broader understanding of big data, its techniques, and its uses.

CHAPTER ONE
How Big is Big?

The tricky thing about quantifying data is that different applications have wildly different demands. Describing the exabytes of data being created daily in terms of how many books could be stacked to the moon and back doesn't resonate with how our brains work.

A million Twitter post histories or Netflix account summaries wouldn't actually take up that much digital space when compared to an Ultra HD video stream with 11 separate channels of high-quality surround sound. However, these simple text records hold a huge amount of potential information. How do we examine and leverage their content in a meaningful way? How do we turn data into insights?

The spread of mobile devices, sensors, and user-created content combined with ever-cheaper storage has encouraged the sheer quantity of data to skyrocket. Some of the leading consumer technology firms responded by simply storing everything possible and keeping an ear to the ground for future use cases. Our focus will be on data with relational and descriptive qualities, as these two things lead to more revealing insights.

"Big data" is a great buzz phrase, but it comes as a bit of a misnomer. Why? Because, at its core, the word "big" is an adjective that highlights the amount of data. "Big data," for our purposes, is better considered a compound noun which speaks to the depth and breadth of the information, rather than simply its quantity. Simply put, we tend to think about "big" data as meaning "lots of data;" however, the "big data" label – as we wish to use it – is better applied to incredibly detailed data.

Whereas we might consider survey results from ten million individuals a "big" set of data, we wouldn't want to call this "big data" without knowing much more about the details. We could certainly call it "large data," or "a big set of data."

Three Vs: Volume, Variety, Velocity

A more fitting application – worthy of the moniker "big data" – would be to see how deep those ten million records go. We're interested in the number of attributes measured within the data set, because we use these attributes to form relationships.

One common description includes the "Three Vs," namely volume, variety, and velocity. Suppose we add more dimensions to our ten million names, with details on age, birthplace, home and work address, favorite color, political affiliation, sleeping position, annual income, etc. Perhaps we update these fields monthly, or even weekly or daily.

Now we have a robust dataset that is broad, deep, and updated over time, with each of these fronts likely to grow as we're able to pull in more subjects to examine. We've achieved big data, and we can start to draw out interesting insights: perhaps we notice that females between 30 and 40 from the Midwest region tend to be side sleepers with high income. Then, because we also have their addresses, we can infer their work commutes so as to position our billboards and advertisements on their exact routes with precise information to boost sales of mattresses.

Before we go too far, though, let's step back and talk more fundamentally about causation and correlation.

CHAPTER TWO
Cause and Effect

What is a causal relationship?

When we start to think of two connected events, we're mentally forming a **causal relationship**. From a purely evolutionary perspective, our brains are wired to look for causation. Our visual system, for example, subconsciously processes mechanical events, such as a moving ball striking a stationary ball, and the movement resulting from the collision. The general idea is that a lack of subconscious, automatic processing by our brains would lead to an extreme energy drain when observing our everyday world. Instead, our brains are wired to observe and retain patterns without re-observing them in a completely new way with each occurrence. Two automobiles are speeding towards each other... well, our brains already know what's about to happen.

Children in the US are very familiar with the following phrase: "If you step on a crack, you'll break your mother's back." This is a very simple illustration of causation – the idea that performing one action directly causes an outcome.

Superstition is also a great (albeit arguably illogical) example of causal relationships. Casino frequenters might claim that a certain machine produces more winnings or that a machine is due to hand out a jackpot simply through personal observation or experience. Statistically, the events are still random – not theoretically but measured and audited by state gaming agencies – but the brain's natural propensity to find patterns to explain cause and effect is quite pervasive.

In today's data-centric world, huge effort is spent harvesting data to reinforce cause and effect. That is, selecting facts to support an earlier narrative, rather than objectively considering all available data. This phenomenon is referred to as **confirmation bias**. If we have a prediction that a large number of accidents are happening at a particular intersection as a result of poor street signage, we may wish to collect data (dates and times of accidents, traffic patterns, deaths) to support the placement of a stop sign. While this makes great intuitive sense, we could easily be wrong.

Instead, we might find that the added stop sign does nothing to affect the number of accidents. The accidents could be the result of the sun blinding drivers as they turn a corner. Here, the true way to reduce the number of accidents would be to alter the intersection or find a solution for the bright sun, but if we never thought to collect that data, we might be stuck force-fitting a story to a narrow view of the facts. Often, this results in wasted time and money. Imagine if we were able to examine all of the data – weather patterns, police reports, the car's engine control unit metrics – from the onset of our investigation.

Traditionally, data is examined through the lens of statistics. We can see examples of this in media headlines: Survey shows 78% of males drink too much alcohol. What we don't see, though, are the reasons behind the effect. We don't see the causes. Frankly, we often can't see the causes, because we don't have the complete picture – we don't have complete data.

Companies are recognizing a changing tide, and they've started to collect data – vast amounts of it – to examine it for new links. The value of data is in its potential uses and the discoveries it might catalyze. Consumers and analyzers of data are shifting from anecdotal causal relationships to the use of data-driven correlations.

CHAPTER THREE
Correlations

Correlations don't rely on cause and effect. Correlations simply imply the existence of a relationship, connection, or association between two or more attributes. Let's do a bit of definition before we go deeper.

When we discuss correlations, each piece involved is formally called a variable, with the input being the **independent variable** and the output being the **dependent variable**. We make or observe changes to the independent variable and note what happens to one or more dependent variables.

When the relationship between two variables maintains movement in strictly one direction (whether positive or negative), they're **monotonically associated**. The relationship between time and age is a monotonic association: As time goes on, our age can only increase.

When two variables are correlated, they can be positively correlated or negatively correlated. If the increase of one variable causes its correlated variable to increase as well, the two variables are **positively correlated**. Age is also positively correlated with time.

In the context of experimentation, we can re-name our independent and dependent variables as the **predictor variable** and the **response variable(s)**. As a simple example, let's assume we collect a set of ages and likelihoods of death. Age (the predictor) and likelihood of death (the response) are positively correlated: as a person gets older, he's more likely to die. Positive correlations can be that simple.

On the other side, if an increase in a variable causes a *decrease* in its associated variable, the two are **negatively correlated**. Maintaining our morose outlook, an increase of time spent exercising (the predictor) might negatively correlate with likelihood of heart attack (the response).

It's also worth noting that correlated variables can change their association; that is, they can change from positively correlated to negatively correlated over time. When this happens, we label the association **non-monotonic**. Speed (the predictor) and miles per gallon (the response) are a great example of this. A car will generally increase its miles per gallon as its speed increases; however, the vehicle will eventually begin to lose efficiency over a certain speed, when losses from wind resistance overtake gains from higher gearing.

Correlation Coefficient

Variables can also be **loosely correlated** or **strongly correlated**. This is a mathematical measure describing the closeness of movement between the two variables. A **correlation coefficient** of zero indicates no relationship and therefore completely random interaction. We'll come back to the calculations later, but values increase toward a maximum of 1 as positive correlation increases, or decrease toward a minimum of -1 as negative correlations increase.

Our positive, monotonic association of age and year has a perfect positive correlation of +1: each additional year of time means one more year of age. It's a one-to-one change. Rainy weather and voting, on the other hand, may have a correlation coefficient of -0.2, indicating a somewhat negative correlation, as increases to one are linked to smaller decreases in the other. It's not a stretch to believe that an increase in rain slightly decreases voter turnout, but we can go a step beyond our hunch and show this mathematically with data.

Now, as we build our statistics toolkit, we can play with these correlations a bit. If we abstract the year into 525,600 minutes, we would say that age and time are very loosely correlated: age only increases once for each 525,600 minutes that elapse. This is a silly scenario, as we know the underlying relationship has not changed, but the scenario is useful to illustrate something we could miss if we didn't know better. Suppose we chose as our sample 10,000 data pairs consisting of a time and an age. With minutes as our time measure, we would see age stay the same for the entire sample, or perhaps change once if we hit a birthday (though this would be unlikely, as 10,000 minutes is only a week). Our conclusion would be that there was zero correlation, or only a weak correlation, between the two, even though we know them to be perfectly correlated.

In addition to being careful to use relevant units and sample sizes or periods, we also must ensure that the relationship we think we've found is statistically significant. Even when variables bear no correlation because they have no impact on one another and do not share a cause, we will always be able to calculate some correlation coefficient in practice. This value may just be so small that we consider it statistically insignificant.

Even when the math shows a correlation coefficient that implies a significant relationship, the leap to causation can be a big one. Websites like Spurious Correlations have intentionally hilarious and absurd pairings, linking Nicolas Cage movies to pool drownings and Japanese car imports to suicides by motor vehicle.

The classic example is the cyclical connection between ice cream consumption and murder rates, which almost certainly do have a relationship. It's not that murderers love ice cream, or that ice cream causes murder, but rather that summer weather has a strong influence on both.

Where it gets more serious, and potentially dangerous, is when the two variables seem to have an intuitive link, or at least some way for us to build a story to explain the correlation ad hoc. Japan has much higher suicide rates than the US, and the rise in Japanese imports wasn't just linked to US suicides in general, but specifically those that occurred by car, so why wouldn't we tend to believe a plausible-sounding explanation? One article claiming Japanese auto design has subtle, depressing cues, or that their new car smell contains a chemical that in large doses is tenuously linked to mood swings, and we would have a viral story that many would accept without the need for rigorous data or further examination. As humans, we've already applied cause and effect to the headline.

If that's too much of a stretch, consider the link between soda consumption and violence in teenagers in Boston schools a decade ago. The math was sound, and the national media enthusiastically reported soda as a leading cause of violence, complete with narratives filled with grave warnings regarding sugar, caffeine, and empty calories. As it turned out, soda consumption was simply a proxy for lower socioeconomic status (lower-income communities drink more sugary drinks), so the true causal relationship was one with SES as the independent variable and both soda & violence as dependent variables.

To take this one step further, many of us would probably agree that removing soda machines from schools should help decrease obesity (in turn, we can imply that the presence of the machines increases the rate of obesity). Data showing unambiguously higher obesity rates in schools with the vending machines would no doubt embolden our belief – yet this also proved wrong! Tracking rates of obesity among students who move between schools with and without vending machines shows that one does not impact the other.

Rather, the schools where soda machines are located are ones where sodas are in higher demand, and the convenient supply does not seem to impact overall consumption (instead, the convenience simply displaces sodas bought elsewhere – like a gas station). Does this mean soda companies are able to locate and target "obese schools?" Probably not; they simply know where sodas are already in-demand based on retail sales. As in the above example, the actual cause for both variables is likely socioeconomics.

Another seemingly plausible – yet incorrect – claim lists divorce as a cause of suicide among men. Overall, divorced men do have a higher rate of suicide, but this is limited to men with a subset of other personality traits and lifestyle variables. These traits are almost certainly contributors to their divorces, but when they are controlled for mathematically, the analysis reveals that divorce itself is not likely a cause of suicide.

Finally, there is the "French paradox" that initially linked high-fat French diets, lower-than-expected cardiovascular disease, and red wine consumption. In the popular press, this morphed into "drink wine and stay thin." That's a hard cause and effect to ignore. Over time, various explanations for the fat-heart link were brought forth, but the wine component proved harder to nail down.

For example, there was the fact that while the French do consume some fatty foods, the rest of their diet is fairly "Mediterranean" and healthy. The original study also took a snapshot of consumption but did not account for the prior decade's runup in fat consumption. In other words, rather than showing a healthy population with an unhealthy diet, the data more likely showed that a recent uptick in unhealthy foods did not immediately negate a lifetime of healthy eating.

But on the red wine consumption side, the correlation remained just that. Moderate consumption did reduce the risk of death from heart attack, but the less acute conditions like general heart health, blood vessel damage, and cholesterol initially linked to polyphenols like resveratrol required impractically large doses.

With so much potential to make false or uncertain connections, how can we definitively prove a relationship? One way is to try to trigger a change in outcome using our suspected causation variable.

Let's Prove It

As an example, much of our medical knowledge begins from observing correlations between input factors (like lifestyle choices) and measuring outputs (such as diseases or health values). After we have inputs and outputs, we can begin to test our observed relationships through **randomized controlled trials** (RCTs).

An RCT involves splitting one group into two groups: a control group and a test population. Then, we apply a treatment strictly to the latter group, the test group, to see what happens. The premise here? If the groups are of sufficient size and randomly chosen, then the impact of unrelated factors that vary from individual to individual will be neutralized, and the only consistent difference between the groups will be attributable to the test drug or therapy.

There is a major limitation to this approach: it can be difficult – even impossible – to test both hard-to-observe and long-duration effects. Additionally, it can be unethical to test hazardous ones... Imagine demanding a rigorous clinical trial to prove that smoking is bad for five-year-olds!

To help overcome challenges related to duration, we can use a related technique: the **longitudinal study**. This study involves sampling outputs over time as the inputs change. Fun fact: The longitudinal study technique was used in the soda example from earlier – after the damage of media hysteria was done, of course. Comparing obesity rates and the presence of soda machines provided a single snapshot and theory, but it was not until follow-up longitudinal studies compared the same individuals moving from schools with machines to those without (or vice versa) that a causal argument could be made, in this case against the idea that soda machines made children more likely to be obese.

Longitudinal studies still require reasonable time frames, easily observable inputs, and sufficient population sizes to control for other variables. We cannot, for example, easily follow thousands of people and wait for some of them to experience a nearby nuclear plant meltdown to compare them to those more fortunate.

Instead, we often settle for correlations, and because they are so much easier to demonstrate, we often see them improperly posed as definitive statements. For example, we might find data to support that lifetime smokers are more likely to develop lung cancer. We might even show that these two variables are strongly correlated. But saying "smoking causes cancer" is sloppy, as not every lifetime smoker will develop lung cancer. Likewise, telling someone that quitting or not smoking at all will prevent cancer is equally short-sighted. If our goal is to get people to recognize the health implications of smoking, both of those causal statements can be undermined, since they invite anecdotal counters: "My grandfather smoked for 60 years and never got cancer, so your claim is incorrect."

The lesson here is to take note of the differences between a correlation that may be random, a proven cause-and-effect relationship, and the murky middle, where there could be a relationship (but it's either unclear what the actual cause is or an attractive narrative has shaped around the data without clear evidence).

If you watch critically, you will find examples of this in the media and also passed on as common sense: rainy weather and damp hair are correlated with catching colds, but neither wet hair nor rain are causes; instead, "cold season" and rainy season happen to overlap.

To summarize this chapter, we've learned that variables can be correlated, either monotonically (via positive or negative correlations) or non-monotonically (by changing directions). These correlations can be the basis for establishing a causal relationship but are not enough to definitively claim a direct cause, and care should be taken to consider alternative explanations, as well as the likelihood of coincidence, before any claims are made. Additionally, the enlightened reader should now begin to dissect the claims made by information providers – there is always more to a claim than what is presented.

CHAPTER FOUR
Methods and Techniques

The main technique for establishing correlations is to run a **linear regression**. The simplest way to picture this is to imagine a grid with two variables as the x- and y-axes. Plotting the points should show some kind of general trend if our chosen variables are correlated. To our earlier example, if x is years spent smoking, and y shows the rate of cancer, we would expect the individual data points to trend upward as we move along the y-axis.

Drawing a line that best fits the data is called regression, and this line allows us to extrapolate new values for regions on the graph where we don't have data. The steepness, or slope, of our line indicates the degree to which a change in the input is expected to affect the output, and we can measure the accuracy of our regression by adding up all the distances between our regression line and the actual data points.

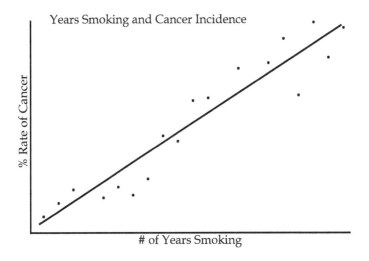

Mathematically, we usually square the distances, making errors increase at a faster rate as they get further from our fit line. This is known as a **least squares regression**, and by penalizing errors more the larger they get, we favor a line that has a bunch of medium-size errors over one with some tiny and some huge errors. If we expect our data to have a normal distribution – that is, to follow the classic bell curve – there should be a whole lot of average errors and few extreme ones.

This technique can also be applied to **nonlinear relationships**, where a change in input does not always have a predictable change in output. For example, cancer risks may only increase slightly for casual smokers, then ramp up dramatically after a certain inflection point when the damage hits a tipping point.

For a simple linear relationship, we end up with a result in the form $y = mx + b$, where y is the dependent variable or output, x is the independent variable or input, m is the slope or correlation coefficient, and b is the error term. Adding multiple inputs for a given output would involve calculating a coefficient for each.

Isn't this just statistics?

So far, none of this is particularly startling research or complex information, but once we start scaling things up, it quickly moves in that direction. One sign that we've entered the realm of big data is when we move from a small number of intuitive, one-to-one correlations to large matrices of correlation coefficients indicating contributions from combinations of variables.

For example, a bank's model of your credit-worthiness might have started as a function of your income, savings, and debt, each assigned a weight that you could readily interpret: income has a strong positive relationship, debt has a negative one, and savings perhaps a somewhat positive, but weaker, input.

In today's big data world, the banks feed dozens – even hundreds – of inputs into a huge regression model. The matrix of correlation values would have many values near zero, indicating that those individual variables don't move the needle much. However, there would likely be combinations of factors that are highly correlated with your individual default risk, whether or not those make intuitive sense. Mathematically, banks may be able to guess when you're ready to splurge on your mid-life crisis, when you're financially preparing for a newborn, and when you send a kid to college. Not from a single decision or action you made, or even several, but from many related measures that explain trends across the broader population. Big data allows companies to tailor a series of variables to predict individual behavior.

With only this explanation, we could draw the line between statistical analysis and big data analysis using quantities of scale and technology: Big data would simply imply "big statistics." This reasoning would leave out many other shifts that come along with big data, from the loss of intuitive relationships in favor of trust in a black box, to greatly expanded types of data we examine, to the marriage of very disparate sets that we think might, when combined, produce new knowledge. And, finally, there is the shift from historically **explaining** behaviors to accurately **predicting** them.

Other Types of Correlations

If the first layer of analysis is demonstrating correlations between variables we suspect to be related, and the second is running regressions on multiple variables to find new relationships, where can we go from there?

One answer is to examine how a set of information relates to itself. Data for financial markets, weather, traffic, and unemployment often exhibits random movement from one point to the next; however, these movements maintain a strong link to prior data points. We call this exploration a **random walk**.

Unemployment, for example, does not jump randomly between values each month, even though the rate of change from the prior month may be random. So, if we're at 5% unemployment this month, next month we might expect to see something in the 4.5% to 5.5% range, with lower probabilities for a plunge below 4% or a spike above 6%, and a jump to 10% would be extremely unlikely. But once we find ourselves at 9% unemployment, a move to 9.5% or 10% would be much more likely than a return to 5%.

This is **time series** data – information whose next values are dependent upon the sequence leading up to them. Should we separate a single series into earlier and later samples, we would find a high degree of **autocorrelation** between the two, indicating that past activity has an influence on future trends.

Whereas we previously tried to fit data to a trend line, when we track autocorrelated data, we calculate a **moving average** to look back a certain number of points and capture a general trend. Since more recent data often has a greater impact, we can also leverage a **weighted moving average** to give new data more influence than older data.

If we want older data to fall away at an accelerating rate, we can limit the average to just a few recent samples or use an **exponentially weighted moving average**. The latter will make data that isn't very recent taper away quickly but without the sharp cutoff we would get by simply excluding it. For example, if most days the markets are calm and then we experience a hard rally or sell-off, each model will react to the new data, but if we drop that point completely after a few periods, we will see a sharp rebound in the output. Letting this response decay away in an exponential fashion will mean its influence drops rapidly but also smoothly.

To reiterate: the move to big data is more than just adding a few extra causes to a common-sense model. In fact, not only are we entering a realm where the equations are not easily explained, but one where we may no longer even wish to – provided we trust our data.

This takes us back to our original description of big data as breadth in addition to depth: the number of records we feed into our regression increases its statistical power, but the breadth gives us a rich combination of interactions that together explain output more accurately than a few handpicked or intuitive parameters would.

Of course, these types of analyses are much more computationally expensive. While more computing horsepower helps, an entirely new set of tools is required once we surpass the limits of Excel and other such "small data" applications. We will talk about new ways to process big data shortly.

CHAPTER FIVE
Where to Start

There are many more complex techniques that can be used to analyze data, but finding and quantifying relationships between inputs is a significant portion of the work. In the context of big data, these relationships require a new set of tools to handle both the quantity of data and the complexity of examination.

Major data-driven firms have mature processes for cataloguing data at the time it is created. For individuals, startups, and incumbent firms looking to take on data initiatives, finding data and getting it into a usable form can be its own challenge.

We could devote the rest of this book to the burdens and obstacles encountered when cleaning big data, so it's hard to overestimate how much work this standardization can take. Even well-resourced organizations spend a lot of time and energy attempting to standardize sets of data, eliminate junk values, and fit disjoint data sets together through a common format. For this reason, some firms pay quite dearly to buy data sets for which someone else has done this arduous work.

Acquiring Big Data

For those without an in-house data repository, the best bet is to find a free and open one. We'll describe a variety of such sources later, but the best scenario is one in which someone else has made a library of clean, standardized data available via a well-documented **application programming interface** (API). An API is an agreed-upon syntax that allows your computer system or application to make requests for data from another system and have it returned in a standardized format.

A web search for "public APIs" will return a variety of open sources, from news and weather around the world to Simpsons quote archives and craft brew data troves. Examples of these APIs are linked at the end of this book for your programming pleasure. There are also a variety of API tutorials available for those who wish to gain familiarity and practice basic commands. Whereas such tutorials typically accept manually-entered commands and display results in a human-readable format, actual programmatic use cases involve coding requests for automatic execution and storing much larger results than are convenient to read on-screen.

In later chapters, we will explore a variety of ways that firms at different scales acquire their data. The acquisition process generally falls into three categories:

• data that is generated in-house, making it proprietary and often a competitive advantage or monetary opportunity;

- data purchased commercially, from specialists who generate or gather it, such as marketing or analytics firms; and

- data from open sources, such as government bodies or non-profit repositories

Storing Big Data

Once the data is collected, which is often an ongoing process, that data must be stored. Here, there are a variety of choices, and some companies have developed innovative file systems specifically designed for storage of big data. Apache's **Hadoop** Distributed File System (HDFS) splits and segments data across multiple storage nodes. Microsoft, too, has entered the storage space and uses its **Azure** Blob storage to provide similar solutions.

Traditional databases are very efficient at storing **structured data**. With structured data, elements fit nicely into rows and columns with appropriate names and types. An example would be a neatly formatted Excel spreadsheet, with the first column containing record counts or perhaps dates, the first row containing column headers for the different pieces of information held, and each individual record subsequently arranged to linearly fit this layout. Often, though, with big data, elements are not as nicely formatted and don't lend themselves to traditional, structured databases.

Information without such a structure is aptly called **unstructured data**. A common indicator is text-based information, such as that generated when scraping raw website data or social media postings. Unstructured data could contain the exact same information as the spreadsheet mentioned above, but instead of neatly segregated pieces of information that can be linked to one another within a single record and compared across other entries, imagine all of our columns collapsed together into a single entry, with no particular ordering.

Specialized database types (such as NoSQL, which we'll describe later) can store unstructured data with ease. In these non-traditional databases, each row of data elements can have its own formatting, column definition, and requirements. Many of these tools, NoSQL included, are open-source and available to use for free.

One irony of "big" data is that, while the method of storage is an important consideration, storage itself is not particularly expensive. The quantity of data being stored has grown, but storage capacity has grown even faster while becoming ever cheaper.

On the lower end, major cloud hosting companies charge around $20 per month (in mid-2018) per terabyte of storage. That terabyte is enough to store hundreds of millions of text records. Attractively, this cost includes the drive itself, the infrastructure, redundancy, availability, power, and cooling. Compared to on-premise configurations, cloud providers allow you to store and retrieve data at will for a fraction of the up-front cost and without any maintenance costs.

On the extreme end of data creation, CERN's Large Hadron Collider is one of the most information-intense pieces of technology in existence. Slamming particles together a billion times per second, each burst generates nearly a petabyte (or 1024 terabytes) of data. Storing all this permanently would get pricey, but as it turns out, the limiting factor is not cost but processing and writing all that data. So, the raw data from the detectors is immediately filtered down to the most relevant information, requiring about one petabyte per day to be stored for further processing.

All told, CERN uses about 200 petabytes (200,000 terabytes) of continual storage. At retail cloud storage prices, this would run about $4 million per month, which is around the same as it would cost to buy that much hard drive storage. Add a bit for the much higher grade of hardware that CERN needs for throughput, subtract a bit for the volume discount they hopefully receive, and then compare it to LHC's estimated $1 billion per year in operating costs. It may not be trivial, but it certainly sounds reasonable.

The lesson here is that storage is a commonly-cited area of challenge; however, it's bandwidth, retrieval, and processing that are often limiting factors to big data applications.

Storing Big Data

After big data is stored, it needs to be filtered and sorted for analysis. **Data warehousing** is the process of compiling and sorting data into logical databases. This can take many forms, and each company or application will likely accomplish this process in a slightly different way.

Before we continue, a few definitions may help to understand the different approaches to data set organization. Taking the structured or unstructured data tables mentioned above, we typically begin with a simple **relational database**, easily visualized as a workbook where each sheet is a table. A **schema** acts as a guide to the database layout, providing rules for how the tables relate.

A **data warehouse** centralizes the various databases within an organization. The warehouse provides a layer above the databases, and this layer is optimized for analytical queries rather than simply writing, modifying, and reading back individual records.

A **data mart** attempts to bring those same analytical efficiencies back down to the individual database level – for example, a data mart could allow for analytics on sales data without requiring a company to optimize its non-relevant manufacturing and supply chain databases.

A **data lake** scales the data warehouse up to "big data" size and handles unstructured data much more efficiently. Instead of meticulously cataloguing and formatting data to fit on metaphorical shelves within the warehouse, we simply dump our unstructured data sets into a lake, with a few basic rules, and allow anyone to go fishing for relevant pieces later. The rules mentioned are in place, and crucial, to prevent the data lake from becoming a dumping ground of unusable data (called a data swamp, just to stretch the metaphor to its limits).

Even if we aren't ready to go as far as a full data lake implementation, we will still want to transform our data to a consistent format as we warehouse it. In general, we want our data to be **time-bound** (that is, related to a specific period of time), static (meaning the data does not change once it is warehoused), and logically relevant to the other material in the warehouse. The rules governing a data lake generally enforce relevancy.

Sorting the data into a data warehouse allows for a more complete view of the data collected. Additionally, it becomes easier to find the data when it is sorted in a consistent manner. From this phase, queries can be constructed to return relevant and consistent results from the data set being managed.

At a basic level, some analytics can be applied to a warehouse of data. Companies have used these techniques for many years: customer segmentation, trend analysis, consumer profiling, etc. Big data analysis, though, aims to uncover new insights through a process called data mining.

Analyzing Big Data

Once the data is stored in a sensical way, analysis can begin. **Data mining** is the process of extracting insights from a set of data. In the same way that physical mining extracts high-value materials from the surrounding ore, data mining must first isolate the signal from the noise before the search for new knowledge can begin.

Until now, we've assumed all our data is relevant and useful, but in many cases, we don't have that luxury. This becomes glaringly apparent when we adapt a broad stream of information to a specific use case. Consider our earlier example of the Large Hadron Collider and its billion collisions per second: Scientists don't actually need that much data for analysis, but the interesting interactions are so rare and impossible to control that the generation of a ton of mundane interactions is procedurally necessary to capture the interesting events. The elusive Higgs boson particle, for example, is produced about once per billion collisions, with around one in five hundred being detected. In precision cases, missing an event or insight would be dramatically more costly than simply storing the entirety of all irrelevant events.

Likewise, a marketing or consumer product firm looking to collect direct customer feedback may mine social media posts on Twitter or Facebook. This **sentiment analysis** requires combing through large amounts of content to find a relevant discussion before further parsing into useful insight.

In these cases, we aren't simply running random regressions; rather, we're looking for specific topics of interest and inferring further information based on nearby data. For example, scraping social media posts, finding specific brand mentions, and then looking for words used nearby to determine customers' impressions.

It's important not to confuse the signal-to-noise ratio with the actual quality of the data – CERN's target data may only be a billionth of the total collected, but its state-of-the-art detectors ensure incredibly high quality. When we combine sufficiently powerful tools (to ferret out the data of interest) and cheap storage costs, we might not care that we started with a million Tweets or a billion collisions to find a target we may have missed otherwise.

For a physical mine, of course, we would prefer finding one solid cube of gold to endless gold dust mixed into tons of rock; however, a major benefit of big data mining is being able to scale up our efforts until we've found enough useful nuggets of information. Once we've isolated the data specific to our use case, we can dive into its relationships and try to draw conclusions.

Often, the analysis stage is divided into two steps: designing a model from existing data, then interpreting its implications for new inputs. This type of model is tweaked and re-calibrated in an iterative process, with the premise that although past relationships or behaviors may evolve, they will do so at a pace that we can track and to which we can adapt our model.

In the case of mining social media posts for opinions, our model would link target topics or brands to categories of words and phrases representing different sentiments. As use of language shifts, we would need to update our vocabulary lists – in fact, rather than trying to maintain rigid categories, we would probably employ the separate discipline of **machine learning** to make those associations. In essence, the computer algorithms could evolve as the languages and phrasing changed.

For the Large Hadron Collider, CERN's model would incorporate speed, mass, and charge of decay products for the protons and lead particles colliding. For industrial equipment maintenance and repair, the model would link combinations of sensor readings to failures or dips in performance.

As part of model validation, a portion of data is typically held back for inspection purposes and to ensure we have not **overfit** the model. Optimizing too far on a given data set effectively force-fits relationships to explain every last detail when we don't actually have enough data to explain everything.

An example of this would be developing a model to explain factors contributing to income. Perhaps our analysis finds university degree and field to be the biggest factors, followed by experience and then school attended, and those values together can explain 85% of income variation.

Depending on how many people we have in these buckets (and what other factors we have information on), that might be as far as we can go.

An overly zealous model may compare you to your nearly identical neighbor and decide the 10k difference between your incomes is determined by how many letters are in your name or something equally nonsensical. The model will be "correct," but only for this specific data set – remember we're just looking for correlations, and long names happen to correlate with higher incomes in our sample of two. Add another person with similar criteria, and the model fails to hold because there's no underlying causal relationship. To error-check, we can apply the model to a portion of data we deliberately held back to confirm whether it is general enough to be used on new data or whether we've overtrained our model beyond its usefulness.

Once we have used our clean data set to build a model, tested it against data not included in the original sample, and confirmed that it is both accurate enough and general enough to give insights on new data, we have to communicate our findings.

Presenting Big Data

As with basic statistical techniques, data presentation is not a new topic, nor one we can properly cover in an introductory text. That said, the advent of big data does present some unique challenges, which we'll describe and for which we'll propose a few solutions.

We can start by going back to the "Three Vs" of big data: volume, variety, and velocity. In the olden days, with a small, static sample, the conclusions reached would be limited in scope and output from a batch, perhaps updating each quarter or month. The "model" or "equation" capturing your findings could be turned into a sentence:

"Women over 25 are 56% more likely to purchase based on our new ad campaign." "Cigarette smoking is the leading cause of lung cancer at the 95% confidence interval." "Each degree the temperature drops decreases our sales by 3%." Add a graph with a couple of key variables, and you have a clear, persuasive story to support your static and time-bound dataset.

Moving into the domain of big data, we quickly run into trouble. Volume itself isn't necessarily a problem, but we may need to deepen our analysis if we introduce more subcategories with sufficient sample sizes that were lacking in prior analysis. With big data, our variety has increased, so we'll be looking at a lot more relationships and generating significantly more complex models that are difficult to explain intuitively:

"Women between 25 and 34, if unmarried, and 22-32, if married, had an increase in purchase rate of 5% per mile from the center of the city in which they lived, but with a drop of 3% per $5k in additional income, unless they were an existing customer, in which case updated percentages can be found in Table 4E…"

As the models become more complex, it may become impossible to distill dozens of interrelated variables into an intuitive summary. Add the third 'V', velocity, and now we're attempting to update this complex mechanism weekly, daily, hourly, or in real-time.

These three layers have fueled the rise of business analytics dashboards which typically summarize insights at a high level but allow slicing and dicing across various criteria to let us wrap our heads around one or two dimensions. The presentation made possible by these dashboards is much easier to process than trying to juggle everything at once.

Qlik and Tableau are probably the best-known generalist tools, and they both adapt quite well to a vast number of different types of data. Many firms also develop their own dashboards to capture specific needs, often using database queries or even Excel/Access as sources of post-analysis data.

The biggest shift here is the interactive component – just as it's difficult to turn a complex model into a sentence explaining cause and effect, capturing the output of our analysis in a single image is a challenge. Being able to step into the data at various layers and see immediate graphical updates as it's explored is much more meaningful.

CHAPTER SIX
Big Data Tools

While some existing technologies were adaptable to the age of big data, new ones were also developed by firms hitting limits and walls. This chapter will focus on some of the more prominent applications and tools, but please be aware that a trove of generic, as well as highly specialized, alternatives exist.

The tools used to extract value from big data can be divided into two categories: tools designed for **storing**, **categorizing**, and **retrieving** massive quantities of data, and applications for **querying**, **analyzing**, and **transforming** it. Following these, we'll touch on a few more tools in the data **visualization** domain.

Storage and Retrieval

The first category focuses on **throughput**. Storage itself has become incredibly cheap, and a variety of technology improvements (such as moving from hard drives to solid state drives and using clever storage indexing techniques) have increased speed. However, the act of finding data in storage, reading it into the computer's working memory, and then writing it back after analysis has physical limits that have been outpaced by demand for ever-larger data sets.

The solution in most cases is parallelism: Simply, data can only flow through the pipes so quickly, so let's make the pipe wider! Another commonly used metaphor is that of the wider highway, with lanes representing discrete processing events, such as queries split among individual servers. Should one piece of the workload or hardware experience a slowdown, traffic in other lanes can continue past it without a bottleneck.

Developed by the Apache Software Foundation, **Hadoop** is arguably the best-known example of this approach. An open-source software library,

Hadoop allows huge data sets to be split across nodes making up a cluster. Built-in redundancy makes data available through multiple nodes at a time, so new requests can effectively pick the shortest line to process quickly.

Previously, big data analysis was only possible with incredibly specialized (and expensive!) computer hardware. The **Hadoop Distributed File System** (HDFS), though, allows scalability to any number of servers, using commodity hardware. By replicating data and related processing tasks across multiple machines, Hadoop allows for some of those machines to fail without compromising the accuracy of output. Whereas an expensive mainframe might fail and lead to severe delays and expensive maintenance, Hadoop combines multiple consumer-grade machines which individually may face higher failure rates, but, when combined, make for a truly robust system.

When a query comes in to retrieve data from this distributed system, a technology called **MapReduce** first determines how best to split the workload among various nodes – this is the "map" piece. It then organizes the data returned from the nodes, with some pre-processing to package it as concisely as possible – this is the "reduce" piece. The combination of parallelization, scalability, and an active developer community streamline both data separation and aggregation.

Cloudera is a leading provider of Hadoop technology, combining the open-source infrastructure with its own services, tweaked for specific use cases. For firms not ready to implement their own Hadoop cluster from start to finish, Cloudera is a popular choice.

MongoDB is another open-source database technology that can scale to big data performance. It sacrifices some of Hadoop's flexibility in exchange for real-time efficiency. Because MongoDB more closely resembles a traditional database, its big data positioning can be viewed as a type of evolutionary upgrade as opposed to the more revolutionary Hadoop-style tools.

MongoDB is considered to be in the **NoSQL** family of database applications. Standing for "Non-SQL" or "Not Only SQL," this type of database strongly emphasizes a distinction from traditional **SQL** (structured query language) relational databases. NoSQL typically prioritizes simplification and the ability to easily scale across any number of low-end systems (called horizontal scaling) as opposed to complex optimization for individual, high-end systems.

Analysis and Transformation

Moving to the analysis side, the categorical emphasis is sheer computational horsepower. As with storage, the exploding demand for deeper analysis has outpaced incremental improvements in speed. Efficiently splitting work into batches that can be tackled in parallel is one solution, but unlike storage (where you can always add another hard drive), upgrading a server's speed typically means replacing it entirely.

Rather than constantly reevaluating expensive step improvements, many firms have outsourced this need to cloud providers. Cloud solutions allow companies to scale hardware demands up and down much more efficiently. Whether run locally or elsewhere, analysis using applications initially designed for limited data sets can become highly inefficient. A new suite of tools has popped up to handle information processing.

A relative of Hadoop, Apache Spark is another open-source tool; however, Spark considers itself a processing system and focuses on executing data analytics in a robust and high speed way. Instead of reading and writing information to hard disks, Spark keeps its data in working memory (RAM) to allow for direct data access at significantly faster rates.

Like other big data storage tools, Spark is designed to spread the workload across a lot of cheap hardware rather than optimize for fixed, high-end devices. Additionally, it is quite fault-tolerant, anticipating a lower level of reliability for individual nodes within its cluster of workers.

There are also adaptations of existing tools to allow them to keep up with the increase in workload. SQL (Structured Query Language) has been one of the dominant database manipulation languages for decades, and tools like Apache **Hive** allow SQL queries against Hadoop storage. Alongside the performance gains from Hadoop storage, Hive has several non-apparent benefits. First, it fits within existing database infrastructure. Second, its technology aligns with the skillsets of traditional database administrators. Newer spin-offs include **MySQL**, a version designed for extremely large-scale web applications (as well as the aforementioned NoSQL, on the storage side).

Beyond prepackaged tools, there are entire programming languages either designed specifically with large-scale data manipulation in mind or adapted for its new challenges. **Python** is probably the language most commonly associated with big data, even though Python proper has been around since 1990. Its combination of simplicity, flexibility, and extensibility encouraged its adoption.

R is another popular language with a focus on statistical analysis and a wide variety of libraries for regressions and modeling. In addition to being able to handle large data sets, R also has built in graphical functions to allow for easier presentation of statistical results without the need for additional tools or plug-ins.

Some of the more general programming languages and tools have been adapted through data-oriented libraries to suit modern needs. Popular examples include Java (due to its maturity level) and **MATLAB** (optimized for matrix manipulation), as well as more specialized languages, like **Scala**, a hybrid language popular for working with financial data.

Data Visualization

Since we eventually need to interpret and act on the results of our analysis, we think it's worth including a few more tools used in presentation.

Qlik, whose main tools include **Qlikview** and **Sense**, has a huge user base across corporate clients who need to perform and present business intelligence. Qlikview is their original software, and specialist users spend substantial time designing the model and anticipating the outputs that business users will want to track over time. Qlik Sense is a more graphics-oriented application, designed to let less technical users experiment and adapt the output to their needs in a more flexible way.

Tableau has probably received more attention than any other data visualization application the past few years, mainly because it offers tremendous flexibility when handling diverse data sources. Tableau requires little expertise to get started, yet it provides a deep level of customization for those who choose to dive in to its functionality at a deeper level. Particularly powerful for presentation is its "Story" mode, allowing users to transition across multiple visualizations in a structured, cohesive way.

R Studio, an interface for the language of the same name, offers a handful of basic charts and plotting functions that can easily be called from within the application. Beyond that, its **Shiny** extension allows easy exports of data presentations to standalone applications, including dynamically generated web content, without needing to code an actual website. This means there is no need to shift skill sets to another application or hand off work to another team, as the same environment can be used for analysis and publishing.

On the more traditional side is Microsoft's **Power BI**. Designed as a corporate business analytics tool, Power BI includes tools for general business intelligence, charting, and dashboard creation, along with a variety of simple add-ons to allow further control over how data is presented. Once an organization has installed Power BI and connected its data sources, the tools within allow for substantial self-service without development expertise, pushing design decisions toward the business users.

On the other end of the spectrum is **Google Charts**. Following Google's trend for application use, Charts aims to be accessible to individual users and smaller organizations, and it includes a set of customizable charting tools online. It also offers many of the dashboards and interactive features of standalone applications, but Charts remain hosted within the Google web app ecosystem while allowing for a variety of data sources as inputs, even dynamic and changing data sets.

On the specialty side of the charting domain is **Datawrapper**, a web-based charting tool targeted at news media and online authors. Accepting data inputs from files or web applications, Datawrapper allows journalists and other types to quickly pick the best presentation format and export column-friendly modules to help tell their stories. By design, it grants users full rights to the outputs they generate, including in commercial settings, only requiring attribution.

There are, of course, many tools across the big data domain, but this sampling covers several of the most widely used tools as well as those with specialized focus. At the very least, if you're hoping to start interacting with big data, we suggest checking out the free, web-based tools, as they require very little in the way of setup and training.

CHAPTER SEVEN
Producers and Consumers

In many cases, the producers and consumers of data are the same players; however, at least for the most sophisticated of firms, some entities stay discreetly on one side of the divide.

Some institutions generate large data sets as part of their mission, while others have expertise in analysis but no direct way to create the data they take as input. We'll try to include a balance of each, but bear in mind that this intro can only hope to cover the tip of the iceberg, and countless firms are on a race to see what new areas of society and business can benefit from having big data tools directed their way.

Most of us are familiar at least to some degree with data generation and its usage by the largest consumer-facing tech firms, if only for reasons of privacy. However, there are many other sources and users of big data, from existing archives being examined in new ways, to incumbent firms leveraging their expertise, to startups helping others make sense of their own processes and systems.

Though the brand-name firms we'll discuss later are some of the best-positioned due to the data generated on their platforms and the resources they have to make use of it, there are open data sources that companies and researchers can access, and key players exist, both large and small, who've been able to carve out a niche in harvesting or interpreting data.

Government and NGOs

Government and NGOs (Non-Governmental Organizations) are some of the most accessible sources for data, especially for those with a research, rather than commercial, data focus. The US Census Bureau and Social Security Administration have demographic data going back decades, much of it freely available for analysis and use. Other government institutions, including the Center for Disease Control, NASA, the NOAA, and the UK's National Health Service, all provide massive data sets to the public.

Additionally, quasi-governmental and NGO organizations such as the World Health Organization, World Bank, International Monetary Fund, and CERN (mentioned earlier, the operators of the Large Hadron Collider) also allow access to their substantial collections for academic and collaborative purposes. Likewise, think tanks including the Pew Research Center, Kaiser Family Foundation, and Rand Corporation are among the dozens with the scale to generate and share data from surveys and other independent research.

On the consumption side, academia and other research-based arenas absolutely dominate. Most of the data generated is not directly monetizable, but by forming the basis for demographic trends, economic developments, and large-scale shifts in behavior, these data sets make their way into commercial models. For many, these data sets provide a great avenue to becoming familiar with large data sets without incurring a cost.

Heavy Industry

Industrial processes and sensors are the next major source of big data generation. Think planes, trains, and automobiles – although the latter can be anything from industrial fleets to huge mining and construction equipment. Key players here include Boeing, Airbus, GE, Honeywell, Caterpillar, Cummins, Komatsu, and Volvo.

Heavy industry is a particularly exciting area, because growth is coming from two very different directions: leveraging existing, often low-tech data streams in completely new ways, and piling on tremendously expanded data sets through higher-tech sensors. Both the miniaturization and commoditization of electronics have made the input sources much cheaper and more sophisticated; thus, companies with investments in expensive equipment have begun to measure everything they can, with incentives identified as reductions in maintenance and repair as well as downtime.

Engine parameters, tire pressures, factory humidity and dust levels, assembly line vibrations, machine tool runout, lubricant quality, particulate count, and nitrogen levels in soil are just a few examples. In many cases, these metrics can be tracked in real time, and this collection works toward our definition of "**smart dust**" (large quantities of low-tech/low-power sensors to be distributed far and wide). Smart dust promises to further reduce the cost of measuring nearly any environmental variable one can think of.

Perhaps the most sophisticated example is that of modern airliners like the Boeing 787 Dreamliner and the Airbus A380, arguably two of the most complex and expensive pieces of equipment in existence. The sensors inside measure thousands of variables and are said to fill an entire hard drive with data from a single short-haul flight.

But surely all this equipment needed to be monitored before sensors became "smart" and ubiquitous, right? As it turns out, there is already a huge base of installed sensors. Some are analog with electronics added later, others take the form of simple checks for whether a measure is within or outside of a tolerance limit, like excessive oil temperature or engine knock detection.

While nowhere near as sophisticated as the newer generation of tools, these present a huge source of data that would either be very expensive to replace or require entirely new equipment to improve. Rather than let better be the enemy of good, companies have dug into this simple data (in many cases nothing more than a zero or one) to see if they can make infer more sophisticated information. By itself, any one data stream would not be considered "big data," but when combined with numerous other "dumb" sensor outputs, the aggregate colors can paint a very dynamic picture.

Uptake and GE are two leading examples. Although one is a budding startup and the other is a multinational conglomerate, both companies have recognized that even limited data from old infrastructure and equipment can be analyzed for warning signs and optimization. Considering the thousands of airliners, locomotives, and other pieces of heavy machinery in use that are 15 to 30 years old, the ability to turn a reading like high oil temperature into actionable insight by combining it with dozens of other low-level pieces of information can be worth millions to the Maintenance, Repair, and Overhaul (MRO) industry.

In GE's case, their knowledge and experience in developing generations of ever-more complex machinery (such as turbofan engines used in jets) have given them a huge database of contextual data to leverage and better interpret the more limited information provided by existing equipment. In Uptake's case, as a pure analytics firms without GE's historical research and development to build upon, they started from scratch and were able to piece together trends by monitoring the operation of such equipment. GE had a wealth of expertise and were probably better able to build the "story" of why certain measurements indicated different conditions, while Uptake is more the "black box" scenario, demonstrating that you do not necessarily need an intuitive explanation if the data is sufficiently deep and trustworthy.

Smart Cities and IoT

If industrial sensors are becoming smaller, lighter, cheaper, and more flexible in their outputs, then it follows that they shouldn't be limited to multimillion dollar, mission-critical equipment. What initially began as companies installing camera networks, integrating door readers, and tracking their supply chains and retail products through cheap, passive **RFID** (radio frequency identification) tags has expanded through the commercial market and onto municipal and consumer markets as the **Internet of Things** (IoT).

Whereas industrial and commercial data are not typically open to outside users, some governments have embraced the potential uses. Initially, the adoption was performed in a closed fashion, analyzing government data to better target services and enforcement. Examples of this include predictive analytics for crimes and code violations through the use of neighborhood trends and comparisons with prior reports.

However, the real potential has been opened up in locations where civil servants have understood they won't likely keep pace with innovation and so have decided to act simply as central sources for information gathering while opening up their repositories for public use. Many urban centers have begun installing sensor arrays on street lights and near intersections to gather environmental and traffic data.

This augments the "traditional" data sources like economic, tax, crime, and energy use libraries, just to name a few. By opening these up to the general public, and even providing APIs for automated retrieval on demand, these data sets have allowed anyone with interest to draw all manner of insights. Transit ridership, building permits, real estate transfers, school performance, and even pet licenses by neighborhood are further examples of data being shared.

As seen with data from national governments and organizations, much of it is better suited for general research and analysis of broad trends. Too, any single source of data may range from simple digitized versions of "small data" to repositories rich with information that can be used to establish all kinds of correlations. As just one example relating to transit, a bus system run on tokens, cash, or disposable passes will provide almost no information aside from ridership assumed from the originating station where the fare was collected.

A level slightly more sophisticated than this example would be a zone-based commuter train, such as Metra Rail in Chicago, which would be able to distinguish riders by distance traveled between zones. Better still would be a system with high adoption of cards linked to individual user accounts, where users "tap in" at the beginning of their route and again at the end of their journeys, such as London's Underground. This simple datapoint adds a tremendous amount of related insight, including source and destination use by station, individual commuting trends, and timing.

Moving past municipal sources, several household names are generating incredible quantities of travel data, to the point they are able to track and predict traffic backups better than local news helicopters. Uber and Lyft have a wealth of data from their drivers, while Waze's navigation platform relies on individual users' real-time application data. In any of these cases, the net-work effect means that each additional user to the system makes the entire system more valuable to all users, so it's only natural that these companies are racing to increase their respective user bases.

Financial Exchanges and Media

Another source of data that has seen an incred-ible increase in both depth and breadth is that of financial, commodity, and derivative markets. Major players in equity markets include NYSE and NASDAQ in the US; the London, Tokyo, Shang-hai, and Hong Kong Stock Exchanges; as well as integrated exchanges such as CME Group, InterContinental Exchange, Eurex, and Deutsche Boerse, each of which hosts trading in commodi-ties and agricultural products, interest rates and other financial products, metals, energy, and derivatives to allow firms to hedge their exposure to weather, crop yields, and financial and geopo-litical risks.

The spread of faster and richer communications media has meant demand for financially-relevant news has skyrocketed, and with it is the demand for markets to react quickly and absorb any spikes in demand. The result has been a move from latency measured in seconds to milliseconds to microseconds (that is, millionths of a second), as brokers seek to offer their customers the best possible price and market makers provide tighter, more competitive spreads.

Estimates put the daily volume of transactions on listed exchanges well beyond 100 million, and into the tens of billions annually, with the number of orders placed a multiple of that. Market data has developed from a simple list of settlement prices to the familiar Open-High-Low-Close (OHLC) structure, and from there to detailed time and sales streams, and this all before the "big data" label became commonplace.

Now, exchanges are expected to provide up-to-the-millisecond order flow information for their most sophisticated customers, who combine it with data from other exchanges and lightning-fast algorithms, seeking to benefit from the tiniest of market inefficiencies. In addition to this, exchanges make available historical market data for backtesting, academic studies, and economic analysis, usually with the basics provided for free and richer data at a price.

The third type of market data is still relatively small from a "big data" perspective but has tremendous potential for the next generation of insight: derived data. This is data from existing markets that by itself may not be actionable but, when tweaked or combined with related sources, becomes the basis for new indices, products, and even funds you may hold in your 401(k) or IRA.

Significant here is the fact that big data analysis can be the inspiration for new derived products, and drawing together multiple sources and translating into a unique output can itself be a source of further big data.

Satellite Imagery

The applications of satellite imagery have grown over the past several decades as image resolution has improved and the number of cameras pointed back at Earth have multiplied. But here, again, big data tools have contributed to a sharp uptick, both in data creation and use.

Landsat, a US government program and the longest running Earth satellite imagery program, has seen private ventures including Planet Labs, Orbital Insight, and DigitalGlobe launch hundreds of their own satellites. These range from the most advanced, with ever-increasing resolution and multi-spectrum coverage, to smaller, modular units that prioritize economy and volume.

Other firms, such as Descartes Labs and Astro Digital, purchase and crunch this data in several novel ways. Precise and timely crop yields, retail sales predictions driven by parking lot capacities, and even energy storage calculated from the shapes of storage tank shadows are three use cases with hefty financial implications.

Finally, non-profit organizations such as the World Wildlife Fund can see whether logging is being done sustainably and track forest loss or regrowth in near-real-time. When natural disasters such as earthquakes or tsunamis occur, their impact to the landscape also becomes visible almost immediately.

Consumer Tech Companies

We started this chapter with a mention of tech firms who've built entire business models around platforms that generate and draw insight from data. The fact that their data is generated in-house, by user activity, within a controlled ecosystem, means they don't have to expend resources buying or creating it, nor do they face competition from others with access to the same data.

These facts also make them incredibly well-positioned to offer additional services, both because of the insight they already have and because those new services will have huge communities from day one. As you can imagine, these two features combine to solidify an arena which becomes very difficult for a standalone service or startup to enter and compete.

So, a simplistic view of Google would look something like this: Google is a search engine company that sells ad space in its search results. Creating Gmail and Google Maps gives them the ability to offer ads in specific contexts, which have a higher success rate and therefore are valued more by advertisers. The Android smartphone software ensures they are the default search engine for an increasingly-mobile society. Finally, the Google Home smart assistant routes more searches to them, improving their core business.

A better, big-data-driven view would look like this: Google wants to map out your behaviors and preferences, from when you ask it for the weather in the morning, to how you commute and what you read on the train to work, to your daily search behavior (and what videos you watch on your lunch break), to the music you listen to at the gym, to what kinds of places you consider for dinner and drinks that evening. Google Home, Android, Gmail, Maps, Music, and YouTube all combine to hand you off from your smart speaker to your phone to your train or car to your laptop.

How about Amazon? The company is an expert at mining purchase data to give you relevant alternatives on their homepage, and its foray into smart speakers and digital assistants could be viewed through the narrow lens of guiding you back to their marketplace. But how do offerings like Prime Video and Prime Music build on that? Perhaps these services get users to the Amazon homepage, where they end up buying things, but that seems tenuous, since people are using mobile and smart TV apps for those services.

Here's an alternative view: Many Amazon customers use Amazon's marketplace for big ticket items, holiday shopping, and other infrequent "batch" orders they complete in front of a computer screen. The experience is similar to a planned grocery run or trip to the mall, and it's definitely not something you do on the go. Since customers may never have a reason to log into Amazon from their phone, every incidental search performed or shared link clicked is lost data (actually worse: it's probably Google's data!).

Including Prime Video, for free, means the consumer might have a reason to log into their Amazon account on a mobile device, whether it's to watch a video at the airport or just to control a smart TV. By doing this just once, those incidental searches and clicked links are now tied to an account. Amazon can pull in order history to put better suggestions on the page, show the One Click button, and perhaps convert customers to "convenience" ordering where Amazon is the source for whatever need pops into your mind on a random Tuesday afternoon.

Even if Amazon doesn't convert the consumer to an immediate sale, that product search will be waiting when the customer arrives home to log in.

This handoff is referred to as the **omnichannel experience**. Maybe you don't really need the motorized tennis ball launcher for your dog that your friend sent you, but instead of forgetting about it, you see it again on your laptop tomorrow and decide to pull the trigger. Spot will love it, you're sure.

One more example: Alibaba, one of the world's largest tech companies, began as a platform for e-commerce, a "Chinese eBay," if you will. Similar to eBay's acquisition of PayPal, Alibaba saw value in taking payment processing in-house and offered Alipay as a new service. Ignoring any strategic "big data" plans, this could've simply been a way to pull customers closer and ensure a third-party payment system did not gain too much influence.

But Alipay gave Alibaba very detailed sales data for transactions on its platform. With such a detailed picture of vendor financial health, they decided they could better assess credit risk than banks. Alibaba launched Ant Financial. Instead of issuing small business loans based on an application representing a single snapshot in time, Ant Financial has ongoing order and payment data. Its algorithms are sophisticated enough to predict delinquencies before they occur and offer extensions or additional credit where appropriate.

Alipay is also a major consumer payment system outside of Alibaba, so again narrowly viewing it as an add-on designed to feed the core business would have been short-sighted. Instead, Alipay's detailed spending data has fueled a move into consumer lending, heretofore limited to established banks.

Alipay goes a step further. Alipay contains third-party services, such as rideshare services and food delivery apps, within its own parent app. In the US, these data-driven firms fight tooth and nail to keep you in their world so you generate more data for them, yet Chinese Alipay managed to envelop them... imagine accessing Amazon's store through Paypal's app, with the latter seeing what you buy directly with the opportunity to leverage that data.

With stores, transit, and other tech-enabled business accepting Alipay, the firm was quickly able to build full financial pictures of individuals as well as businesses. The natural next step was to launch Zhima Credit. This was seamless to the user, who didn't have to download it because it appeared automatically in the Alipay app. Zhima Credit began offering discounts and down payment reductions to a variety of credit-linked services based on its knowledge about users' financial habits.

As details of what went into these next-gen credit scores surfaced, including unpaid parking tickets and the scores of one's friends, and ways in which it could be limiting to those with inadequate scores, such as restrictions on higher tiers of travel services, fear spread that this could become an all-encompassing "good citizen" score, with no choice for anyone but to participate. Awareness has spread, debates have raged, and pushback is emerging, but these services bring up a variety of questions regarding privacy, sharing of data, and what individual users can or should do in response...

CHAPTER EIGHT
Privacy, Tracking, and "Defensive Data"

A "social credit score" that punishes you for being friends with the wrong people or for a hundred other unknowns sounds terrifying… or are we just being paranoid? Of course, big data can be used for malevolent and Orwellian purposes, but how real is the threat? And is there a middle ground between tossing your phone out and moving to the mountains and surrendering every intimate detail of your life?

Those are big questions with a lot of complexity, but we'll try to give some condensed, practical answers. For some context, your authors consider themselves reasonably tech-savvy, with substantial experience working for tech-enabled firms. We view technology overall as a force for good, with some reservations about information overreach.

Am I Being Followed?

Let's start with the difference between personal and aggregate data. Anything you do without logging in to a service is aggregate data – individual websites still harvest that, but they aren't linking it to you personally. Anything behind a login is being used to paint a picture of who you are and what you do in order to bring you more of what they think you'll use. Separately, any method of electronic payment is being mined, either to detect fraud, figure out what credit cards and other offers to send you, or evaluate your broader credit and financial situation.

Where this topic gets tricky is in the level of connectivity across devices and the web. If you're logged into Google, Facebook, Amazon, or other service, that data is linking back to your profile. This means smart TVs and watches, but it also encompasses the use of your social media login to comment on third-party news articles, play games, or check in to events. If you're using Google,

Samsung, or Apple Pay, the data for those transactions goes far beyond your banking relationship.

Our suggestion here is to view connectivity across platforms in moderation: do you really need to log in to Facebook to comment on a local news article? It may certainly be convenient, but it's convenient at a cost. The cost is your data. If you're a heavy user of Google services, have you tried Firefox as your web browser? Do you benefit if the company with your web history also gets your payment history? How much of your digital life would be disrupted by losing access to a single service?

Beyond diversifying your data footprint, there are some simple steps to limit how much data others can gather about you. Most users are familiar with the use of software such as **Ad-Block Plus** to cut down on intrusive ads that often follow your online activity, but there are a few others that also block tracking scripts and aim to prevent your activity elsewhere from getting back to the mothership. These include **NoScript**, **Privacy Badger**, and **Ghostery** as browser extensions. You can also install the **Ad-Block Plus Browser** on your phone to keep your searches and web use contained.

Finally, most modern browsers have a Privacy mode which throws away any cookies or temporary files once you exit that window – the convenience you lose may not be worth the privacy savings, but we suggest giving them a try for a day to see just how often you find yourself logging into something. This provides a great demonstration of just how much of your activity is normally linked through the services you stay permanently logged into. To start a Privacy session, use *control-shift-N* in Chrome or Opera, or *control-shift-P* in Firefox or Internet Explorer.

Metadata

How do you track someone without snooping? You use data about data, without ever looking at the actual data itself. There has been a ton of discussion in the last few years about government surveillance, in large part due to the amount of data it was gathering without actually listening to calls. As it turns out, tracking patterns in when and how someone communicates can paint a very detailed picture without the need to view the actual information (which comes with all kinds of pesky legal restrictions).

But this also has a friendly side: Google can piece together your commuting habits and provide you with helpful information like your ETA without needing you to engage in a bunch of manual setup. It simply builds a pattern around your phone's location and what it discerns is your typical work day, customizes it to your particular schedule, and from there, it can warn you about traffic delays and upcoming weather, or even meal specials at the restaurants it assumes you're heading to after work.

The reality is this: if you own a smartphone, you're constantly sending out sonar-like pings of your location. Assuming you aren't the subject of a criminal investigation, the uses by mainstream firms are mostly benign. Additionally, location services are difficult to avoid, since they're so deeply embedded in the iPhone and Android operating systems. Did you know that Airplane Mode doesn't turn off GPS? And for modern phones, powering them "off" usually just puts them into a standby mode. Phone cases with integrated **Faraday cages** are available, blocking electromagnetic signals in and out more thoroughly than turning off the phone.

Barring extreme cases, the potential concern for most users is third-party applications, which may pull data from any number of sensors and could potentially include personal data rather than just anonymized statistics. Both of the major operating systems attempt to control this by requiring user permission for access to potentially sensitive data, but it's easy for users to gloss past this screen. Have you ever read the terms and conditions?

Mainstream applications get a lot of scrutiny, but it may be worth a few minutes of your time to go through the more obscure ones and see if anything looks odd, like that tip calculator you installed that has access to your microphone and camera. On Android, click *Settings, Apps & Notifications*, then, within an app, choose *Permissions*. On Apple's iOS, tap *Settings* and select an app.

Consumer Protection Legislation

We've left legal protections for last, due both to skepticism any law will keep up with the ingenuity of those wishing to gather data and the fact that bad actors will ignore laws in part or in whole. With that said, there are a few policies of note that set some ground rules around the collection and use of data.

In the United States, the two areas with the most protection of personal data are healthcare and credit, with **HIPAA** (Health Insurance Portability and Accountability Act) and **FCRA** (Fair Credit Reporting Act) requiring end user permission for sharing of data. Beyond those and a few smaller, industry-specific restrictions, it's very much a case of buyer beware, so those long user agreements may be worth a closer look to see what you're allowing them to do with your data.

In the European Union, a recent attempt was made to curb the excesses of private data use via the General Data Protection Regulation (**GDPR**). Specifically geared toward personally identifiable information, these regulations require explicit permission from the end user for a multitude of data considerations. Built-in rights, such as the Right to be Forgotten (formerly called Data Erasure), for example, give end users the ability to request removal of personal data and halt further dissemination – one case at a time (how many digital companies do you interact with?). The Right to be Forgotten is just one example in a very complex set of regulations.

Unfortunately, the strict requirements of GDPR proved difficult for many online services to implement. Due to the time crunch and operational complexity, many services opted to simply block users from the European Union. On the other end of the spectrum, many of the big tech players simply presented a screen asking for permission to use any and all data before users could continue to their websites.

Similar to the pesky software license agreements, many users will blindly accept just to remove the glaring pop-up. The end result of a law trying to rein in the biggest players may simply overwhelm their smaller competition while having everyone agree to the same level of data collection as before.

So again, caveat emptor...

CHAPTER NINE
Benefits and Prediction

Now that we've covered topics of concern with data use, it's a good idea to highlight the positives as well. In particular, this closing chapter will focus on forward-looking applications. Predicting the future – although imprecise – is more exciting than simply describing the past. In earlier chapters, we mined our data, established correlations, and measured how input contributions shape our outputs. Now, what can we do with our findings?

We've discussed a bit about the insights available when examining massive data sets. But we haven't yet looked at the potential for real-time analytics. Not only can companies infer new information, they can do so in near-real-time. As events happen, potential outcomes can be predicted with shocking accuracy. And with computing power continually on the rise, companies are able to process more data at even faster speeds.

Anecdotes like Target's prediction of a girl's pregnancy before her father knew, and the quest for the perfect recommendation algorithm (Amazon, Netflix), have become ancient examples as big data practitioners have turned their sights on innovative new uses.

It is every company's dream to accurately predict future behavior from past performance, and the trail of digital breadcrumbs that our phones leave throughout our day to day lives have received the lion's share of recent attention.

As consumers, we find value in knowing how long our commutes will take. If one company provides that service more accurately or more reliably, we'll tend to use that company. Google Maps has done a great job understanding what its users want. We can see static data, like how many miles away our destination is; calculated information, like the number of minutes in current traffic; and immediate information, such as the level of busyness at your destination. Integrating this information with its review system, Google also shows the thoughts, experiences, and feelings of other customers.

Health organizations can use big data to predict disease outbreaks and the velocity of their spread. Farmers can leverage big data insights to predict and control for weather pattern changes. Even everyone's favorite villain in the internet age, advertising, can use its analytical powers for good. By tracking response rates to different ads, advertisers can tailor what you're shown much more quickly than in the past. While these efforts won't cut down the number of ads you face, most consumers will find their ads more relevant – and, in some cases, helpful – as the data is supporting individual user behavior rather than broadly-defined demographic groups.

This doesn't just mean using your search history to serve up more customized responses. Major websites routinely perform **A/B Testing** by presenting different layouts or new features to different users randomly, measuring the response to create a better experience.

Fraud detection has moved from looking for obvious outliers, like purchases from outside the country, to highly accurate predictions based on user behavior including purchase size, type of item, time of day, and day of the week. Distributed weather services, such as WeatherSignal, take a distributed approach to weather mapping by collecting and merging real-time mobile data at the individual level. Instead of relying on individual weather stations, which may not be representative, WeatherSignal's approach greatly broadens access to information.

Municipalities can track water and power use in real-time and predict upticks during critical shortages. Commonwealth Edison, in Illinois, uses a similar approach to curtail energy use by providing billing credits to subscribers lowering their energy consumption during peak hours. Traffic signal timing can be adjusted in a coordinated fashion and throughout changing situations, while inspectors and first responders can be deployed to higher-likelihood areas to better stretch limited resources.

Businesses can run server farms and office building climate control with input from other sites to increase efficiency and reduce cost. Fitness tracking applications can turn a routine heart rate, step count, or sleep chart into actionable insights based on patterns from thousands of others.

The common theme to most of these applications, and the reasons the exceptions leave us uneasy, is the ratio of benevolent helpfulness to visible intrusion. Or, as one colleague put it, "I appreciate it when you help me, just don't be creepy about it." Where you draw that line may be a matter of taste, in the "I'll know it when I see it" category, and companies playing in that region have seen pushback.

CONCLUSION

We hope you've enjoyed *That Book on Big Data: A One-Hour Intro*. We trust that we've armed you with a solid definition of "big data" as well as an understanding of its promise and future applications. Should you wish to peel back the next layer of the onion, we've provided some of the more interesting resources we referenced. You'll find these in the next chapter.

We've also included a vocabulary list – many of these topics easily warrant their own books, but given their ubiquity in discussions on big data, we think there's inherent value from having a basic understanding of each. Our recommendation is to skim through and brush up on any topics you find intriguing.

Finally, if you have feedback, we'd love to hear it! You can reach us directly by email:

authors@thatbookonbigdata.com

Should you feel so inclined, we'd love to have your candid and honest review on Amazon. Whether we earned your five-star review or landed somewhere else, your feedback is critically important for the next reader looking to pick up our book.

Thank you for choosing to spend your time learning with us. Take care!

ADDITIONAL RESOURCES

Articles

After Privacy Concerns, Zhima Credit Admits it
was 'Stupid'
http://www.sixthtone.com/news/1001503/af
ter-privacy-concerns%2C-zhima-credit-admits-
it-was-stupid

Blakemore SJ, Fonlupt P, Pachot-Clouard M,
Darmon C, Boyer P, Meltzoff AN, Segebarth C,
Decety J.

CERN Data
https://home.cern/about/updates/2017/07/c
ern-data-centre-passes-200-petabyte-milestone

CERN/LCH guide (pp. 35, 50 for collisions)
http://cds.cern.ch/record/2255762/files/CER
N-Brochure-2017-002-Eng.pdf

Inside China's Vast New Experiment in Social
Ranking
https://www.wired.com/story/age-of-social-
credit/

Is Soda a Smoking Gun for Teen Violence – Or Just
Statistical Illiteracy?

https://www.forbes.com/sites/trevorbutterw orth/2011/11/02/is-soda-a-smoking-gun-for-teen-violence-or-just-statistical-illiteracy

Neuroreport. 2001 Dec 4;12(17):3741-6.

No Safe Haven: Diet Sodas Linked With Health Risks
https://www.reuters.com/article/us-heart-softdrinks/no-safe-haven-diet-sodas-linked-with-health-risks-idUSN2339241420070723

Soda and Violence. Harvard Magazine.
https://harvardmagazine.com/2012/11/soda-and-violence

Spurious Correlations, by Tyler Vigen
http://www.tylervigen.com/spurious-correlations

The Race to Rule the High-Flying Business of Satellite Imagery
https://www.wired.com/2017/03/race-rule-high-flying-business-satellite-imagery/

Websites

Brewdog Beer API
https://punkapi.com/documentation/v2

News API
  https://newsapi.org/

Open Weather Map API
  https://openweathermap.org/

Simpsons Quote API
  https://thesimpsonsquoteapi.glitch.me/

Whitepapers

Beyond the Hype: Big Data Concepts, Methods, and Analytics
    by Amir Gandomi, Murtaza Haider
    https://www.sciencedirect.com/science/article/pii/S0268401214001066

VOCABULARY

A/B Testing – an experiment involving the random presentation of alternative versions (A and B) of a service or website while collecting information on user responses to each

Application Programming Interface (API) – a standardized way for applications to request data

Autocorrelation – correlation between a data set and a translated version of itself, usually time-shifted, which indicates earlier samples have an impact on later ones

Confirmation bias – selectively noticing new information that matches an existing belief, while discarding contradictory info

Correlation – a relationship between two variables where movement in one corresponds to movement in the other

Correlation Coefficient – a mathematical measure describing how closely two (or more) variables are related, ranging from 0 for no relationship to -1 or +1 for complete dependency in either direction

Data Lake – a method of storing data without a complex hierarchy and often without a fixed structure, allowing flexible retrieval for many uses

Data Mining – analyzing a collection of data to find new insights or usable subsets

Data Swamp – a data lake that has become a dumping ground of unusable data

Data Warehousing – the process of compiling and sorting data into logical databases. This is the step prior to data mining

Database – a set of stored data with a defined structure, usually across multiple dimensions, for selective retrieval

Exponentially Weighted Moving Average – a moving average where more recent values have significantly higher weights before rapidly dropping off as new data is created

Faraday Cage – an enclosure of metallic mesh with openings small enough (relative to the relevant wavelength) to act as a conductive sphere which blocks electromagnetic signals

FCRA – the Fair Credit Reporting Act, a 1970 US law regulating the transfer of personal financial information

GDPR – the General Data Protection Regulation, a 2018 EU law governing the use and sharing of personal data, particularly with respect to technology companies online

HIPAA – the Health Insurance Portability and Accountability Act, a 1996 US law regulating the transfer of personal medical information

Internet of Things – the growing collection of networked "smart devices," including appliances, cameras, and sensors that communicate alongside computers and smartphones

Least Squares Regression – similar to linear regression; however, non-conforming data is penalized heavily to minimize large outliers

Linear Regression – using an equation to extrapolate new output values when assuming input values that matched the original data set

Longitudinal Study – longer-term studies used to observe and infer results from several samples taken over time

Loosely Correlated – two variables are not strongly tied to the changes in each

Machine Learning – a highly iterative process by which computers categorize and model input data to achieve target outputs, without specific human-created rules

Metadata – "data about data," such as the time, size, and recipient of a call or email without the actual content

Monotonically Associated – in a correlation, meaning two variables always move in the same direction (positively or negatively)

Moving Average – an average applied to a subset of data, typically in sequence; for example, a rolling 30-day average for a stock market index

Negative Correlation – an increase in the predictor variable causes a decrease in the response variable, or the other way around

Nonlinear Relationships – a relationship between two variables where a change in the predictor does not always produce the same amount of change in the response

Non-Monotonically Associated – in a correlation, meaning two variables do not always move in the same direction (they can switch from positively correlated to negatively correlated)

Omnichannel – a seamless user experience across multiple platforms, such as desktop, mobile, and smart device, particularly with respect to technology companies

Overfitting – a condition whereby a statistical model has optimized for a specific sample set to the degree that it explains random noise, losing predictive power for other data sets

Positive Correlation – an increase in the predictor variable causes an increase in the response variable, or the other way around

Predictor Variable – in a correlation, the influencing variable

Random Walk – a sequential process where each new sample is not a random value, but a random distance from the prior value; for example, a stock's price movements

Randomized Controlled Trials (RCTs) – an experiment whereby a group is split in half randomly, with one half receiving a treatment and the other not, with the results observed; with sufficient size in each group, unrelated factors cancel out

Response Variable – in a correlation, the variable being influenced by the predictor variable

RFID – radio-frequency identification, a low-power, short-distance communication method used for touchless tracking of assets and other objects

Schema – an overview of the structure of a particular database, used to locate items in subsequent queries

Sentiment Analysis (Opinion Mining) – examination of human-generated text, often from social media posts, to identify the mood, tone, or reaction toward a given topic

Smart City – a city which integrates various datasets and interconnects municipal systems to provide better information and improve services, including traffic, finances, crime, permitting, ordinances, weather, events, and utilities

Smart Dust – cheap, disposable, low-power sensors designed to be deployed indiscriminately into environments that are difficult for higher-tech ones to reach

Strongly Correlated – two variables are tightly bound in their movement (i.e. a large increase in one implies a large increase in the other)

Structured Data – data entries that fit nicely within a set of static rows and columns

Throughput – the amount of data that can be processed or analyzed at a time

Time Series – used to describe a set of data where the next values rely on prior, historical, values

Unstructured Data – data that does not fit a consistent layout, often consisting of unordered text generated by human input

Variable – an individual piece of data used in a correlation

Weighted Moving Average – a moving average where values have different contributions to the result, typically with more recent samples counting more heavily